Lerner SPORTS™

WORLD CUP FAN GUIDES

ENGLAND NATIONAL SOCCER TEAMS

ULTIMATE FAN GUIDE

JANIE SCHEFFER

Lerner Publications ◆ Minneapolis

To Dad and Katie—you will always be my Pelé and Mia Hamm.

Lerner Publications Company
An imprint of Lerner Publishing Group, Inc.
241 First Avenue North
Minneapolis, MN 55401 USA

For reading levels and more information, look up this title at www.lernerbooks.com.

Main body text set in Aptifer Slab LT Pro. Typeface provided by Linotype AG.

Editor: Matt Doeden **Designer:** Viet Chu **Photo Editor:** Lucien Brinkley
Lerner team: Sue Marquis

Library of Congress Cataloging-in-Publication Data

Names: Scheffer, Janie, 1992– author
Title: England national soccer teams : ultimate fan guide / Janie Scheffer.

Description: Minneapolis : Lerner Publications, [2026] | Series: Lerner Sports. World Cup fan guides | Includes bibliographical references and index. | Audience: Ages 7–11 | Audience: Grades 4–6 | Summary: "Focusing on the men's and women's national soccer teams, this book covers the history of soccer in England. Learn more about memorable moments, key players, and the vibrant fan culture that surrounds soccer in England"—Provided by publisher.
Identifiers: LCCN 2025013353 (print) | LCCN 2025013354 (ebook) | ISBN 9798765689400 lib. bdg. | ISBN 9798348029326 pbk | ISBN 9798765698709 epub
Subjects: LCSH: European Championship (Soccer tournament) | World Cup (Soccer) | Soccer teams—England—History—Juvenile literature | Soccer—England—History—Juvenile literature
Classification: LCC GV944.E5 S35 2026 (print) | LCC GV944.E5 (ebook) | DDC 796.334094—dc23/eng/20250813

LC record available at https://lccn.loc.gov/2025013353
LC ebook record available at https://lccn.loc.gov/2025013354

Manufactured in the United States of America
1-1012738-54808-8/13/2025

TABLE OF CONTENTS

A record number of fans pack Wembley Stadium in London, England, for the 2022 Euro.

INTRODUCTION

HOME FIELD CHAMPIONS

On their home field, England's women's soccer team battled in a tough match against powerful Germany. It was the 2022 Women's European Championship (Euro) final. The score was tied 1–1 in extra time.

England's forward Lauren Hemp kicked the ball to teammate Lucy Bronze. Bronze kicked it toward the front of Germany's goal. There was a crowded frenzy in front of the net. After missing a chance to knock the ball in, forward Chloe Kelly got another shot. This time she was ready. Kelly tapped the ball into the back of the net. Goal! England's players swarmed the field to celebrate their 2022 Euro championship.

Men's and women's national soccer teams are made up of the country's most talented players. For both men's and women's teams, the biggest title to earn is the World Cup. This competition is organized by FIFA and is hosted by different countries every four years.

FAST FACTS

The England men's team is called the Three Lions, and the women's team is called the Lionesses.

England's men's team played for the first time in 1870.

England's women won the 2022 Women's Euro in their fiftieth year as a team.

England's men won the 1966 World Cup title at home against West Germany.

Forward Chloe Kelly bangs in the game-winner at the 2022 Euro final.

Beyond the World Cup, many national teams also compete in the Summer Olympics every four years. Men's and women's national teams from Europe also play in the Euro tournament every four years. England has one of the longest-standing soccer histories in the world, and its players and fans are proud to carry on the legacy.

England celebrates their championship at the 2022 Euro.

England's men's team trains before a match in 1930.

CHAPTER 1

A LONG TRADITION

In 1870, England's first men's national team faced off against Scotland. It was the world's first match between national teams. They ended the match in a tie, 1–1.

England's men's team became known as the Three Lions for the lion images on their uniforms. The team went on to play for many years in the British Home Championship tournament against British club teams. The national team first won the title in 1888. In 1900, England played in the first Olympic Games to include soccer. They won the gold medal. Their Olympic success continued in 1908 and 1912 as the Three Lions won gold both times.

England's 1938 team poses before a match with Ireland. England went on to win 7-0.

Defender Jack Charlton (*center*) goes for the ball against Siegfried Held of West Germany in the 1966 World Cup final. Charlton's brother, Bobby, also played on the team.

Until 1966, the team had little success at the World Cup. But that year, England was hosting the tournament. Superstars Bobby Moore, Bobby Charlton, and Gordon Banks led the way as England finally broke through to win the championship. In the years since, England's best World Cup finish was fourth in 1990 and 2018.

England's men have also found success in the Euro. As the host team in 1996, England made it to the semifinals against Germany. The teams had a fierce rivalry. The match was decided by penalty kicks. England's dream of winning it all on their own field ended when Germany's goalkeeper saved the final shot.

Forward Alan Shearer (*right*) controls the ball at the 1996 Euro.

A similar ending came in the 2021 Euro final when England lost to Italy in penalty kicks. Three years later, under the leadership of coach Gareth Southgate, England made it to the final once again. It was a hard-fought match. England midfielder Cole Palmer scored the team's only goal. It wasn't enough. They lost to Spain 2–1. England finished as runners-up once again.

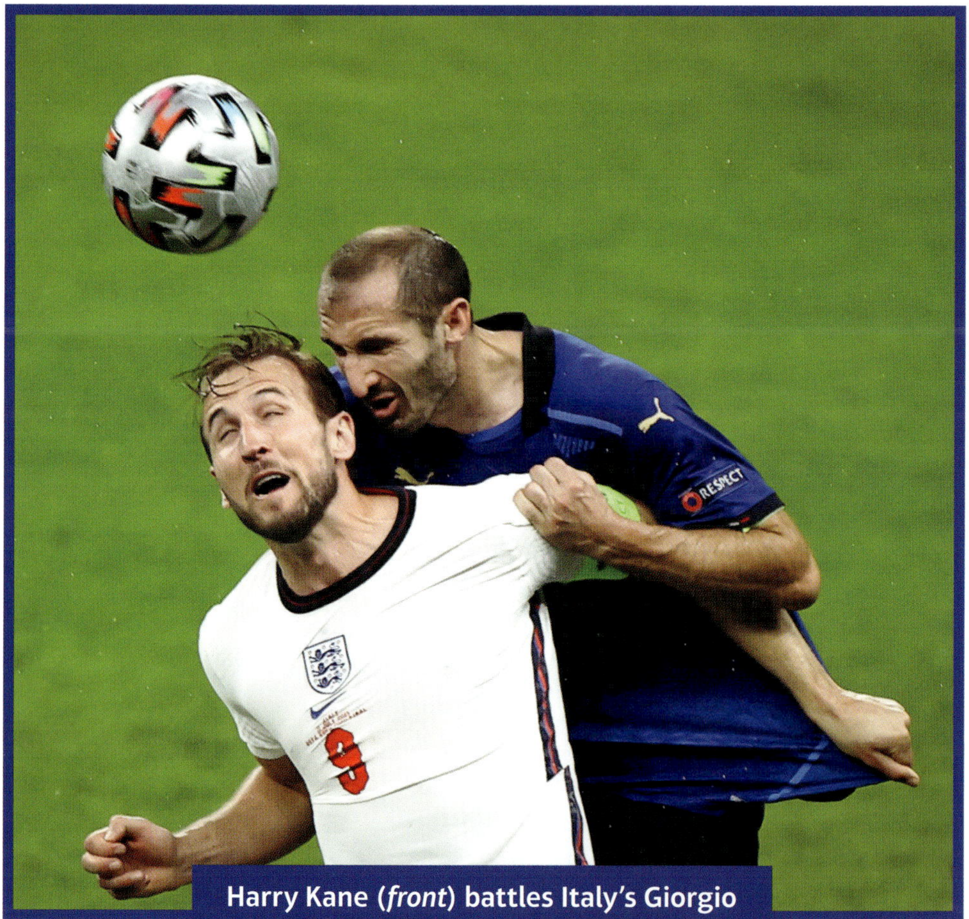

Harry Kane (*front*) battles Italy's Giorgio Chiellini for the ball at the 2021 Euro final.

England's women's team formed in 1972.

The road for women's soccer in England has been bumpy. In 1921, England banned women from playing on most pro soccer fields. For 51 years, girls and women did not have the chance to play in organized soccer programs. The ban ended in 1971.

In 1972, England's first women's team, the Lionesses, played an official match against Scotland. The game itself and the Lionesses' victory were both breakthroughs. Women's soccer in England grew over the next decade.

The Lionesses kept improving. In 1984, they finished in second place at the Women's Euro. In 1985 and 1988, they won an international tournament called the Mundialito. In 1988, a newspaper named them Team of the Year. In 1995, England made its first appearance in the Women's World Cup.

Hope Powell was a key player for England at the time. As a midfielder, she scored 35 goals in 66 caps wearing the Lioness jersey. In 1998, Powell was named the head coach of the Lionesses and led the team for the next 15 years.

Hope Powell (*center*) goes for the ball in a match with Germany.

Alex Greenwood (*right*) makes contact with Spain's Salma Paralluelo at the 2023 World Cup final.

The Lionesses' biggest win came at the 2022 Euro. They beat longtime rival Germany 2–1 to win the championship. The Lionesses have continued searching for World Cup glory. The team returned to the World Cup in 2007, 2011, 2015, 2019, and 2023. Their 2023 appearance was their best. The team beat Australia 3–1 to advance to the final. But Spain ended their hopes, winning 1–0 to take the World Cup.

INCREASED SUPPORT

The 2022 Women's Euro was played at Wembley Stadium in London in front of 87,192 fans.

Striker Geoff Hurst (*left*) scores a goal against West Germany in the 1966 World Cup final.

CHAPTER 2

MAGICAL MOMENTS

England's men have played in 16 World Cups. Their first was in 1950. England's only World Cup title came in 1966 at home. In a packed Wembley Stadium, manager Alf Ramsey led the Three Lions to victory against West Germany in the final. With one minute left to play and England ahead by one goal, West Germany tied the game 2–2. But England bounced back. Striker Geoff Hurst scored two goals in extra time to secure the World Cup title.

With a total of three goals scored in the match, Hurst became the first player to get a hat trick in the World Cup final. Defender and captain Bobby Moore was another key part of the team. Most other players of the era, including the legendary Pelé, called Moore the best defender in the world.

Bobby Moore (*left*), Geoff Hurst (*middle*), and Martin Peters (*right*) celebrate their title at the 1966 World Cup.

England's Lionesses have played in the Women's World Cup six times. During their first appearance in 1995, the team lost to Germany.

In 1996, England's men hosted the Euro. A highlight of the tournament came when England beat longtime rival Scotland 2–1 in the group stage. England thrilled fans by making it to the semifinals.

Midfielder Paul Gascoigne (*left*) holds off a Scotland defender at the 1996 Euro.

Fara Williams winds up for a penalty kick at the 2015 World Cup.

In 2015, England's women made another World Cup run. They reached the tournament's third-place game, where they faced Germany. England's Fara Williams scored on a penalty kick in extra time to give England the victory.

One of the men's team's most exciting World Cup matches came in 2018. The team made history when it defeated Colombia in penalty kicks. Harry Kane, Marcus Rashford, Kieran Trippier, and Eric Dier all scored on their attempts. It was the first time England had ever won a World Cup game in penalty kicks.

COLLECTING CAPS

Peter Shilton's 125 caps hold the record for England's national team. Wayne Rooney and David Beckham hold the second and third spots with 120 and 115 caps.

In 2021, the Three Lions finished as the runners-up in the Euro. England's captain and all-time top scorer Harry Kane scored a rebound goal in extra time to beat Denmark. England advanced to the final but lost to Italy.

Harry Kane scores a goal in the 2020 Euro.

Forward Beth Mead controls the ball at the 2022 Euro.

It was the women's turn at the 2022 Euro. Forward Beth Mead led England's charge to the championship. Mead was the top scorer of the tournament with six goals and five assists. She was named Player of the Tournament. It was the biggest win yet for the Lionesses. It was also their 50th anniversary of being a national team.

In the 2023 World Cup, the Lionesses faced Australia in the semifinals. Ella Toone, Lauren Hemp, and Alessia Russo scored goals for England in a 3–1 victory. The team went on to finish in second place, losing to Spain in the final. England's Mary Earps was awarded the Golden Glove as the top goalkeeper of the tournament.

England's men returned to the Euro final in 2024. The match was tied 1–1 in the closing minutes. But Spain scored a late goal to claim the title.

Goalkeeper Mary Earps makes a save in the 2023 World Cup final.

The party is on outside Wembley Stadium before the 2020 Euro final.

CHAPTER 3

STILL GROWING

England was one of the inventors of soccer. Along with Scotland, the Three Lions are one of the oldest national soccer teams. As the English men's and women's programs have grown, so have the fan bases. The Three Lions's fans have been filling Wembley Stadium since 1923. The Lionesses' supporters began packing Wembley Stadium in

Fans pack the stands at a 1996 Euro match between Germany and England.

2014. That included a crowd of almost 90,000 people to see the women win the 2022 Euro final!

In the past, a small number of England's fans have made news for their bad behavior. Called hooligans, these fans sometimes disrupt the game for others. The problem has grown smaller in recent years, but some fans still get out of control.

CONSTANT CONTENDERS

The Three Lions have competed in every World Cup except 1974 and 1978. The Lionesses have missed only 1999 and 2003.

Most fans come to games only to support their team. England's fans are known for their chants and songs before, during, and after matches. Some chants and songs are in support of specific players. Others, such as the popular "We're on our way!" chant, cheer on the whole team.

Young soccer fans are decked out in England gear for the 2023 Women's World Cup.

Soccer players often start young in England. There are many chances for kids to play at all different levels. This boosts the talent on both of the national teams. Fans also cheer on pro club teams in the Premier League and the Women's Super League. Some of the biggest stars on the national teams also play in the Premier League and Women's Super League.

Children practice soccer in northeast England. The sport is a way of life for many people in the country.

Kostas Tsimikas (*left*) of Liverpool fights for the ball against Harry Howell of Brighton in a 2025 match.

England's teams have a bright future. Fans can't wait to see how they do in future tournaments. The men's team hopes to qualify for the 2026 World Cup. Meanwhile, the women look ahead to the 2027 Women's World Cup.

ENGLAND MEN'S SOCCER TIMELINE

1870 England's men tie with Scotland in the world's first international soccer match.

1888 The Three Lions win the British Home Championship.

1900 England wins its first Olympic gold medal in soccer.

1966 The team wins the World Cup title.

1996 The team makes it to the semifinal game of the Euro.

2018 England finishes fourth in the World Cup.

2021 England places second in the Euro.

2024 The team again finishes second in the Euro.

ENGLAND WOMEN'S SOCCER TIMELINE

1972 England's women play their first official match.

1984 The Lionesses finish second in the Euro.

1985 The team wins its first Mundialito title.

1988 England wins their second Mundialito title.

1995 England plays in its first World Cup.

2009 England finishes second in the Euro.

2015 Fara Williams scores on a penalty kick to give England third place in the World Cup.

2022 England wins the Euro in front of their home fans.

2023 The team finishes second in the World Cup.

GLOSSARY

cap: an international game played

captain: a player who is the official leader of a team

club team: an amateur or pro soccer team that is not a national team

extra time: time added to the end of each half in soccer

FIFA: a group that oversees soccer around the world

group stage: the stage of a tournament in which teams in a group play one another

hat trick: three goals scored in a game by one person

midfielder: a soccer player whose main jobs are to pass the ball and defend

penalty kick: a free kick at the goal allowed for certain fouls or to decide the winner of some games

rivalry: a fierce competition between two teams

semifinal: a game or a series of games coming before the final round in a tournament

striker: a soccer player who usually stays near the other team's goal

LEARN MORE

Britannica Kids: World Cup
https://kids.britannica.com/kids/article/World-Cup/390872

Goldstein, Margaret J. *Women's Professional Soccer.* Lerner Publications, 2026.

Kiddle: Football Facts for Kids
https://kids.kiddle.co/Football

Scheff, Matt. *The World Cup: Soccer's Greatest Tournament.* Lerner Publications, 2021.

Sports Illustrated Kids: Soccer
https://www.sikids.com/tag/soccer

Streeter, Anthony. *World Cup All-Time Greats.* Press Box Books, 2025.

INDEX

PHOTO ACKNOWLEDGMENTS

Image credits: Daniela Porcelli/SPP/Sipa USA via AP Images, p. 4; Julian Finney - The FA/The FA via Getty Images, p. 6; Lynne Cameron - The FA/The FA via Getty Images, p. 7; Imagno/Getty Images, p. 8; Daily Herald/Mirrorpix via Getty Images, p. 9; Rolls Press/Popperfoto via Getty Images, p. 10; Lutz Bongarts/Bongarts/Getty Images, p. 11; Christian Charisius/picture alliance via Getty Images, p. 12; Ronald Dumont/Daily Express/Hulton Archive/Getty Images, p. 13; PA Images/Alamy, p. 14; Quinn Rooney/Getty Images, p. 15; Hulton Archive/Getty Images, p. 16; Paul Popper/Popperfoto via Getty Images, p. 17; Richard Sellers/Sportsphoto/Allstar via Getty Images, pp. 18, 24; Dennis Grombkowski/Bongarts/Getty Images, p. 19; Laurence Griffiths/Pool Photo via AP, p. 20; Jonathan Moscrop/Getty Images, p. 21; AP Photo/Abbie Parr, p. 22; Wiktor Szymanowicz/NurPhoto via AP, p. 23; Patricia Pérez Ferraro/SOPA Images/LightRocket via Getty Images, p. 25; SolStock/Getty Images, p. 26; AP Photo/Ian Walton, p. 27. Design elements: Ralf Hiemisch/Getty Images; Rifqyhsn Design/Getty Images; cunfek/Getty Images; poo worawit/Getty Images.

Cover: Action Foto Sport/NurPhoto via AP; David Klein/Sportimage/Cal Sport Media via AP.